DK READERS

Level 2

Dinosaur Dinners
Fire Fighter!
Bugs! Bugs! Bugs!
Slinky, Scaly Snakes!
Animal Hospital
The Little Ballerina
Munching, Crunching, Sniffing,
  and Snooping
The Secret Life of Trees
Winking, Blinking, Wiggling,
  and Waggling
Astronaut: Living in Space
Twisters!
Holiday! Celebration Days
  around the World
The Story of Pocahontas
Horse Show
Survivors: The Night the Titanic Sank
Eruption! The Story of Volcanoes
The Story of Columbus
Journey of a Humpback Whale
Amazing Buildings
Feathers, Flippers, and Feet
Outback Adventure: Australian Vacation
Sniffles, Sneezes, Hiccups, and Coughs
Ice Skating Stars
Let's Go Riding
I Want to Be a Gymnast
Starry Sky
Earth Smart: How to Take Care
  of the Environment

Water Everywhere
Telling Time
A Trip to the Theater
Journey of a Pioneer
Inauguration Day
Emperor Penguins
The Great Migration
Star Wars: Journey Through Space
Star Wars: A Queen's Diary
Star Wars: R2-D2 and Friends
Star Wars: Join the Rebels
Star Wars: Clone Troopers in Action
Star Wars: The Adventures of Han Solo
Star Wars The Clone Wars: Jedi in Training
Star Wars The Clone Wars: Anakin in Action!
Star Wars The Clone Wars: Stand Aside—Bounty
  Hunters!
Star Wars The Clone Wars: Boba Fett: Jedi
  Hunter
WWE: John Cena
Pokémon: Meet the Pokémon
Pokémon: Meet Ash!
LEGO® Kingdoms: Defend the Castle
LEGO® Star Wars®: The Phantom Menace
Meet the X-Men
Indiana Jones: Traps and Snares
¡Insectos! en español
¡Bomberos! en español
La Historia de Pocahontas en español

Level 3

Shark Attack!
Beastly Tales
Titanic
Invaders from Outer Space
Movie Magic
Time Traveler
Bermuda Triangle
Tiger Tales
Plants Bite Back!
Zeppelin: The Age of the Airship
Spies
Terror on the Amazon
Disasters at Sea
The Story of Anne Frank
Abraham Lincoln: Lawyer, Leader, Legend
George Washington: Soldier, Hero, President
Extreme Sports
Spiders' Secrets
The Big Dinosaur Dig
Space Heroes: Amazing Astronauts
The Story of Chocolate
School Days Around the World
Polar Bear Alert!
Welcome to China
My First Ballet Show
Ape Adventures
Greek Myths

Amazing Animal Journeys
Spacebusters: The Race to the Moon
Ant Antics
WWE: Triple H
WWE: Undertaker
Star Wars: Star Pilot
Star Wars: I Want to Be a Jedi
Star Wars: The Story of Darth Vader
Star Wars: Yoda in Action
Star Wars: Forces of Darkness
Star Wars: Death Star Battles
Star Wars: Feel the Force!
Star Wars The Clone Wars: Forces of Darkness
Star Wars The Clone Wars: Yoda in Action!
Star Wars The Clone Wars: Jedi Heroes
Marvel Heroes: Amazing Powers
The X-Men School
Pokémon: Explore with Ash and Dawn
Pokémon: Become a Pokémon Trainer
The Invincible Iron Man: Friends and Enemies
Wolverine: Awesome Powers
Abraham Lincoln: Abogado, Líder, Leyenda en
  español
Al Espacio: La Carrera a la Luna
  en español
Fantastic Four: The World's Greatest Superteam
Indiana Jones: Great Escapes

A Note to Parents

DK READERS is a compelling program for beginning readers, designed in conjunction with leading literacy experts, including Dr. Linda Gambrell, Distinguished Professor of Education at Clemson University. Dr. Gambrell has served as President of the National Reading Conference, the College Reading Association, and the International Reading Association.

Beautiful illustrations and superb full-color photographs combine with engaging, easy-to-read stories to offer a fresh approach to each subject in the series. Each DK READER is guaranteed to capture a child's interest while developing his or her reading skills, general knowledge, and love of reading.

The five levels of DK READERS are aimed at different reading abilities, enabling you to choose the books that are exactly right for your child:

Pre-level 1: Learning to read
Level 1: Beginning to read
Level 2: Beginning to read alone
Level 3: Reading alone
Level 4: Proficient readers

The "normal" age at which a child begins to read can be anywhere from three to eight years old. Adult participation through the lower levels is very helpful for providing encouragement, discussing storylines, and sounding out unfamiliar words.

No matter which level you select, you can be sure that you are helping your child learn to read, then read to learn!

LONDON, NEW YORK, MUNICH,
MELBOURNE, and DELHI

For Dorling Kindersley
Managing Art Editor Ron Stobbart
Publishing Manager Catherine Saunders
Art Director Lisa Lanzarini
Publisher Simon Beecroft
Publishing Director Alex Allan
Production Editor Marc Staples
Production Controller Kara Wallace
Reading Consultant Linda B. Gambrell, Ph.D.

For Lucasfilm
Executive Editor J. W. Rinzler
Art Director Troy Alders
Keeper of the Holocron Leland Chee
Director of Publishing Carol Roeder

Designed and edited by Tall Tree Ltd
Designer Ben Ruocco
Editor Jon Richards

First American Edition, 2012

12 13 14 15 16 10 9 8 7 6 5 4 3 2

002-182941-May/2012

Published in the United States by DK Publishing
375 Hudson Street, New York, New York 10014

DK books are available at special discounts when purchased in bulk
for sales promotions, premiums, fund-raising, or educational use.
For details, contact:
DK Publishing Special Markets
375 Hudson Street
New York, New York 10014
SpecialSales@dk.com

A catalog record for this book is available
from the Library of Congress.

ISBN: 9780756692452 (Paperback)
ISBN: 9780756692445 (Hardback)

Printed and bound in China by L. Rex Printing Company Ltd

Discover more at
www.dk.com
www.starwars.com

DK READERS

BEGINNING
TO READ ALONE
2

STAR WARS

THE CLONE WARS

Chewbacca
and the Wookiee Warriors

Written by
Simon Beecroft

Have you met Chewbacca?
Chewbacca is a Wookiee.
He comes from a planet
called Kashyyyk.
He is tall and strong and his
body is covered with hair.

Wookiee words

Chewbacca can understand our words.
But he can't speak them, because his
mouth cannot make the sounds.
He can only speak the Wookiee language.

Sharp teeth

When he
speaks,
Chewbacca
shows his
sharp teeth
and growls!

It is not a good idea to upset
Chewbacca. He might try to
pull your arm off!

Bowcaster

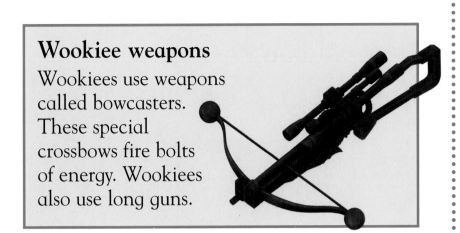

Wookiee weapons
Wookiees use weapons called bowcasters. These special crossbows fire bolts of energy. Wookiees also use long guns.

Chewbacca trained as a warrior. He has a ferocious temper and great strength. But he is usually friendly.

Wookiees are very intelligent. They build cities in the tall trees on their planet. They fly starships through space. They are also really good at fixing spaceship engines.

How old do you think Chewbacca is? Chewbacca is nearly 200 years old! But that's quite young for a Wookiee. Wookiees can live for more than 600 years.

Jedi student
Ahsoka Tano is a Jedi student, called a Padawan. The Jedi are warrior monks who use a mysterious energy called the Force to increase their powers.

Look at how much
taller Chewbacca is
than Ahsoka!

Fully grown
Wookiees
are much
taller than
most humans.

Tarfful is Chewbacca's friend.
He is a Wookiee chieftain.
He and Chewbacca have fought
side-by-side in many battles.

During the Clone Wars, Tarfful
and Chewbacca defended their
world from a deadly droid army.
Like Chewbacca, Tarfful is
calm and thoughtful.
But in battle, he is ferocious!

The Clone Wars
The Clone Wars were a
huge conflict in the galaxy.
Deadly droid armies invaded
many worlds and tried to take
them over by force.

Trandoshans are the Wookiees' deadly enemies. Trandoshans are large reptiles and their skin is covered in scales. Their hands and feet have three razor-sharp claws.

Old enemies
Wookiees and Trandoshans live on nearby planets. In the Clone Wars, the Wookiees support the Jedi and the Trandoshans support the droid armies. This makes them sworn enemies.

Trandoshans are warlike and
dangerous. They like to hunt
and capture Wookiees for fun.

Trandoshan hunters release captured Wookiees and other species on an isolated forest moon called Wasskah. Then they hunt the captives on the moon, just for fun.

Hunting Speeders

Trandoshan hunters use hunting speeders to chase after their prey. The speeders are armed with powerful cannons.

Once, some
Trandoshans
captured a group of Padawans,
including Ahsoka. They took
them to Wasskah. Ahsoka hides
from the Trandoshans under
a tree. Can you spot her?

Ahsoka and the Padawans spot a Trandoshan spaceship. They leap onto the top of the spaceship before it lands. They battle their way inside the spaceship.

Ahsoka surprises the pilot
with a flying Jedi kick!
But watch out! Now no one
is steering the ship...

The Jedi leap from the ship just before it crashes. The ship also has a prisoner, locked up in a cage. When the ship crashes, the cage opens, and the prisoner walks free. It is Chewbacca!

Ahsoka and Chewbacca realize
they can help each other.
Chewbacca tries to mend the
crashed ship's transmitter
to call for help. But he cannot
get it to work.

The Jedi Padawans have an idea. They capture a Trandoshan hunter and use their powers to control his mind. They tell him to call the other Trandoshans and ask to be picked up.

A hunting speeder appears.
Our heroes hide until the
speeder reaches
the mind-
tricked
Trandoshan.

When the speeder is close,
Ahsoka leaps high in the air
and kicks out the pilot.
She then jumps out after him.
On the ground, the pilot gets
up to fight Ahsoka.

He thinks she looks easy to beat.
But he's wrong...

Ahsoka is a well-trained Jedi.
She also has a Wookiee for a
friend! Now it is the pilot who
looks up, because Chewbacca is
so tall. The pilot is not so sure of
himself now!

Chewbacca bashes the pilot.
One bash from Chewbacca is
enough to knock out the pilot!
Chewbacca and the Jedi fly off
in the Trandoshan speeder.
It's time to escape this moon!

Our heroes spot a Trandoshan fortress floating in the clouds. The Trandoshan guards are surprised to see a hunting speeder arrive with a Wookiee and three Jedi on board!

Floating fortress

The Trandoshan hunters' base is a floating fortress. Inside, the Trandoshans display the creatures they have hunted.

Chewbacca and the Jedi fight the guards. Suddenly, one of the guards makes a loud screeching noise. He is calling for help.

Trandoshan guard

More Trandoshan guards arrive.
They are armed with blasters.
The Jedi use the Force to knock
the guns out of their hands.

Chewbacca wrestles with one of the guards, while the Jedi fight the others.

More guards appear.
They overpower Chewbacca and the Jedi. Oh no!
The Trandoshans have defeated our heroes.

Just then, a spaceship arrives. Tarfful and a team of Wookiee warriors are on board. The transmitter did get a message to the Wookiees after all!

After a battle, Chewbacca and the Wookiee warriors finally defeat the Trandoshans.
At last, they can leave the moon!
Victory is theirs!

Future hero
We will see Chewbacca again. He will be a great Wookiee warrior in many battles during the Clone Wars and afterward.

Quiz

1. What is the name of the Wookiee planet?
2. How long can Wookiees live?
3. What does Chewbacca try to fix on the crashed Trandoshan spaceship?
4. What is the name of Chewbacca's Wookiee best friend?

Put the scenes in the right order:

A

B

C

D

Answers: 1. Kashyyyk, 2. 600 years,
3. A transmitter, 4. Tarfful
The correct order is C, D, A, B

Index